soft in the middle

shelby eileen

to those who thought they were made of peach pits,

mountain ranges, oak trees, and

difficulty

only to realize they were made of all those things

+ ocean waves, feathered wings, 10,000 shades of pink, and

softness

soft in the middle

shelby eileen

content warnings:
negative body image
blood
sex
emotional abuse

*When it comes to **these feelings**, maybe I should have paid more attention to dates and timelines and whether the words were born to be sorted. I don't have categories for them. I don't know if they were meant to express themselves in a certain way. I just know they wouldn't leave me alone for months. I coaxed the feelings out of my mind by the roots because, no matter how much I wish it weren't so; I am just a girl, not a garden. They bloomed too furiously for my own being to handle. I forgive them for that.*

there is just their body
and then their afterthought

body

there are so many words I've left unsaid
so instead of going another year or five or ten
in brutal, crushing silence
don't waste this opportunity
don't be scared when the full weight of my heart
tests the strength of your hands
I'm trusting you with something I barely trust myself with
this knowing
this telling
this momentous uprooting
I'm here
I am
I am right here in these words

I think
if I have ever loved you
that means that I'll be on your side
always

this has happened before
I have said
"I love you"
and
"I trust you"
and
"when we're together"
and
"..."
they either leave me or never get the chance to
because I leave them first

these words are what I'm saying when I say nothing at all

between me and the people I love
something always breaks, or fades away
hearts come undone like strings of pearls
feelings disappear like earrings
by now my jewellery box is almost empty

is this the reason
I've never liked
wearing stones and silver
at the same time?

there is always too much to lose

I had a dream
that your eyes locked on mine
and you leaned right into me
and kissed me on the lips
kissed me so slow and so sweet
like honey moving between teeth

you can talk like you're in love with a person
without really knowing them at all
you can picture a thousand different futures with them
like you can picture your mother's eyes
and your favourite mug
you can make things out to be so familiar
things that don't even exist

(I've done it)

she's something more like mountain air
and rivers you could bathe in, drink from, float down till the
end
she's something more like droplets of rainwater
you open your mouth to catch
because of how sweet and delicate it feels
to have her on your tongue

she looks up at the night sky
and often finds that what she sees
is what she feels inside
when the stars float brightly, she thinks

breathing is like swimming
            the water holds me so gently
                    the weight of everything
                        is easy to hold

when the clouds cloak the world in darkness, she thinks

                    it's getting harder
            to dream
        of possibility

everything is always happening; trying and doing and falling
and failing
life is never still

God, I feel free
because I don't feel empty
without you all the time
-anymore

how do you tell a stranger
you think you could love them forever?

similarly

how do you tell the one you love
you think you'd be better off without them?

I don't know how to articulate heartache
it's not something that's ever happened to me
not really
how do you mourn the loss of a love you never spoke out loud
never
felt with your own two hands?

I resent how goddamn rare it is
that I feel loved, honestly
but then I remember
how very moving it is
that I honestly feel loved
at all

and if I can't be loved, I hope I can be let go
like petals on the wind
and horses running home

your eyes are so beautiful
through them, I bet the world is tinged with gold

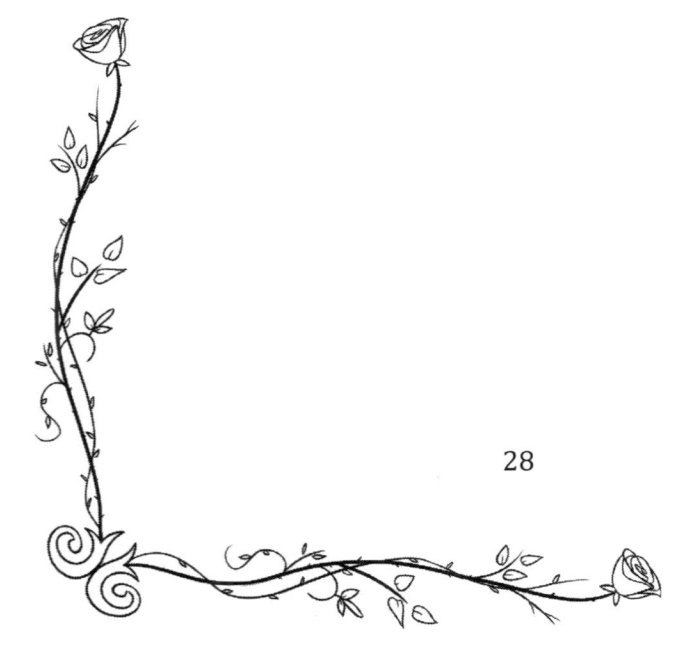

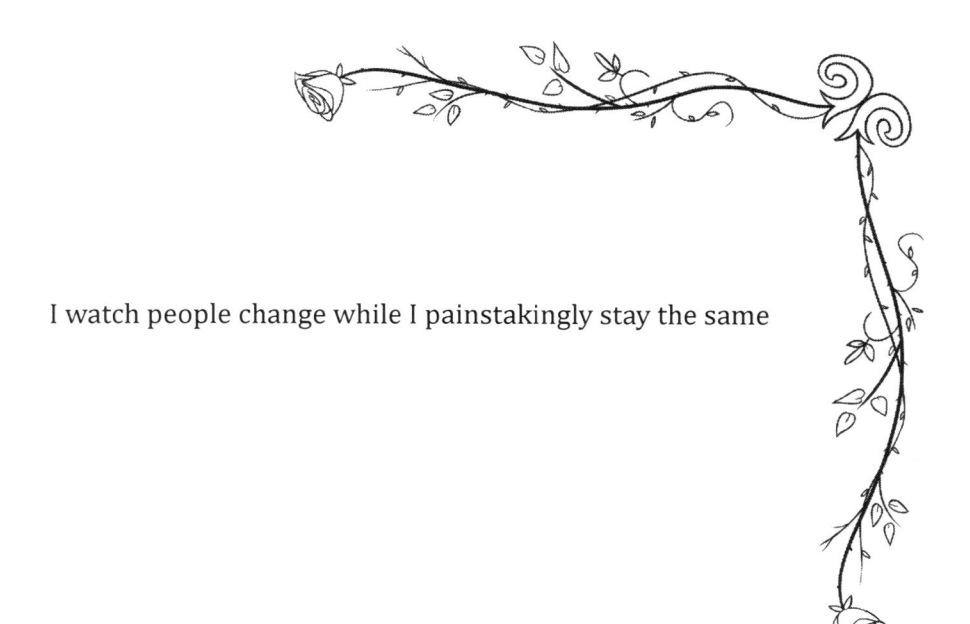

I watch people change while I painstakingly stay the same

some subjects are best put to rest
when your words reach for
scalpels
more often than
sutures

I know that probably neither of us wants to admit that the reason we don't talk as much anymore is because we've run out of things to say to each other. Things that are allowed. Things that are appropriate. It hurts so much that words would betray us this way.

it really doesn't matter if I lose a few pounds
or 10 or 20 or 30
what is 30 pounds of ice off a glacier?
when my mother says, "I think you've lost weight"
I don't let it feel like a compliment
anymore
because no matter what I lose
I'll never lose enough
and if I lose enough
I'll have lost everything

Just because the risk is important and difficult, it doesn't convince the stars to align. Perhaps they had other hearts to draw together at the time you reached out to them. Perhaps if you ask them again somewhere down the line, they won't be so busy. Perhaps your questions and answers will be completely different. The stars will always be there, but you should move forward.

does anything I say
mean anything at all?
when it rains
how important is each droplet?
any drop
could swell to spill
every word
helps me breathe

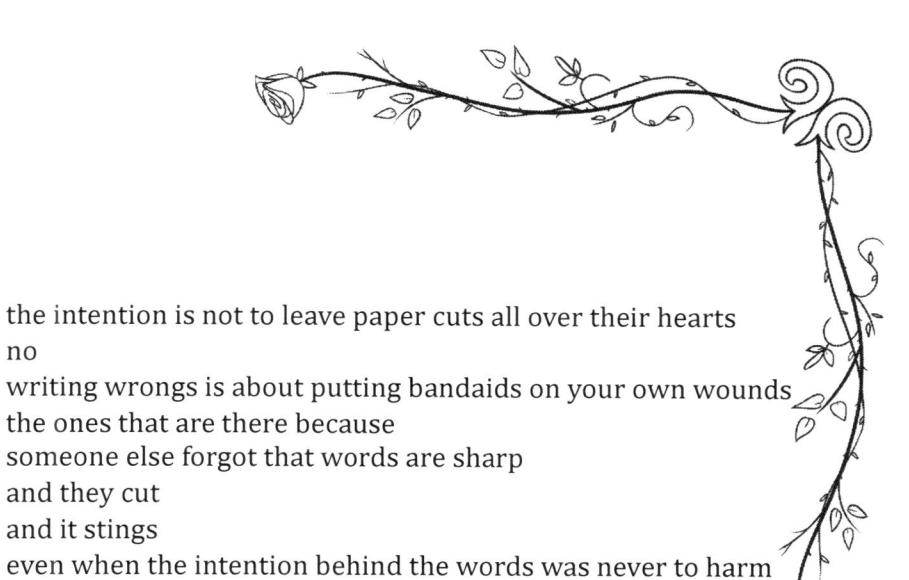

the intention is not to leave paper cuts all over their hearts
no
writing wrongs is about putting bandaids on your own wounds
the ones that are there because
someone else forgot that words are sharp
and they cut
and it stings
even when the intention behind the words was never to harm

you could lay yourself completely bare on the table-
with your worst fears on this plate here
and your wildest dreams in that bowl there
but they're just not hungry

no one ever seems to be hungry for you

I ruin everything I touch
and boy do I know the shape of my own body well

I can't look at beautiful things
because every beautiful thing
reminds me of you

maybe now
instead of going out of my way to show you beautiful things
hoping they'll make you think of me
the way they make me think of you
I'll take the time to appreciate those things-
I'm worthy of being a witness to beauty
the stars shine for me too

no one will ever love me
perhaps someone is capable
but surely I'll stop them
before they ever get too close
making my own misery is what I do best

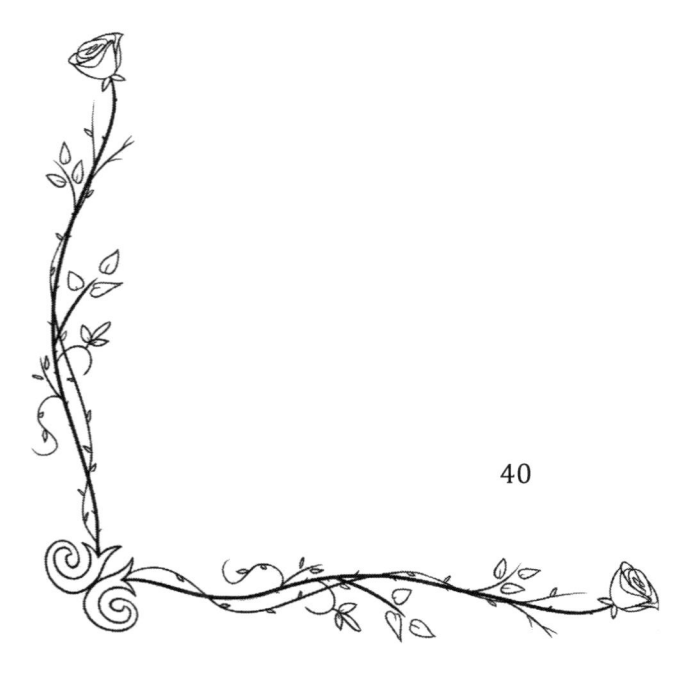

I am huge
there is too much of me,
and not in a good way
- from the girl whose favourite animals are whales, and bears,
and elephants

when I'm frustrated
I wish you'd never cared about me at all
I would rather that than this;

feeling like I was high on your words
when I'd never done a drug in my life
feeling seen and heard and worthy
feeling too much
feeling raw
overcome
pushed to the edge

of   a

crest   wave

a long,

brutal

fall

down

she was whoever she wanted to be
however she wanted to be
and most of the time
she just happened to be
soft and sexless
singing always
studying sunshine
so as to become as lovely as its light

I stepped into the ocean
with my whole life clutched in my hands
the current took this
and swept away with the tides went that
for every thing that I had lost
I tried to find something in the swirling depths to take its place

so my fistful of dirt
was replaced with a pearl
watery fingers loosened ribbons from my hair
and wove, instead, a constellation of stars there

I knew from that first step I took
forward into the water
arms overflowing with temporary possessions
that I would win some
and
lose some

what have we done
to get this way?
what have we done
to feel like this?

like we're sitting at the bottom of the ocean
sunken like anchors
weighted like grief

if we reach out, we can almost touch
if we speak, we might catch muffled sound

but I just can't seem to hold you
and words have been dying just behind my lips,
and the things we are still sharing
are but stale crumbs
of what was once
so tender

I don't feel warm in your words anymore

does he respect you?
does it feel nice when he puts his hands on you?
these answers have to match
-this is what it feels like to be dragged through fire

I feel myself becoming a cave;
curving around my centre
hardening to protect
what sometimes makes me feel hollow

[you breathe]
[I collapse]

the world stacks the cons of being soft
but that doesn't stop me
from reaching for the clouds
while embodying them too

what do you want from me
and my glass heart
you, carelessly putting your fingerprints all over me
at least have the decency to leave me clear
for the next people to look inside me
won't be able to see through the smudges and handling of past
hands
and this will no doubt
cause them to turn away quickly
move along briskly
you don't stare too long into a window
when there's only darkness on the other side

Thumbing through old poems I wrote when I was sad about you is like dipping my fingers in acid, and swallowing it too. I hate feeling those things again. I hate realizing that I was wrong. I didn't move on. Those feelings were just frozen and now they're thawing; spilling and messy; staining and toxic; harsh and hollow.

I don't want a great many things from life
so the things that I want
that I can't have
break my heart the most

I keep
inside me
an inventory of things
that I regret I've shared
and who I've shared them with
it's not that they weren't worthy
it's that I don't know how to give myself up
so easily

every minute
of every day
in every thought
that I can't stop thinking
I feel the limitations on me
questioning whether the way I'm living
-and loving-
is ok

it is my desire to hold your hand
to cradle your cheek
to stroke your hair
to give you the world

BRAVURA

it's like you woke me up
made me see sunsets
in every pair of brown eyes
none compare to yours
all the rest are beautiful too,
it's just that yours are made of
pure starlight

do you hate that I like you?
does it hurt that I love you?
would it be best if I thought nothing of you?
my brain just loves to turn diamonds back to coal

you are a bouquet crafted by artisans
you are a garden inspired by Eden
not one leaf is set by way of accident
not one petal curves by way of chance

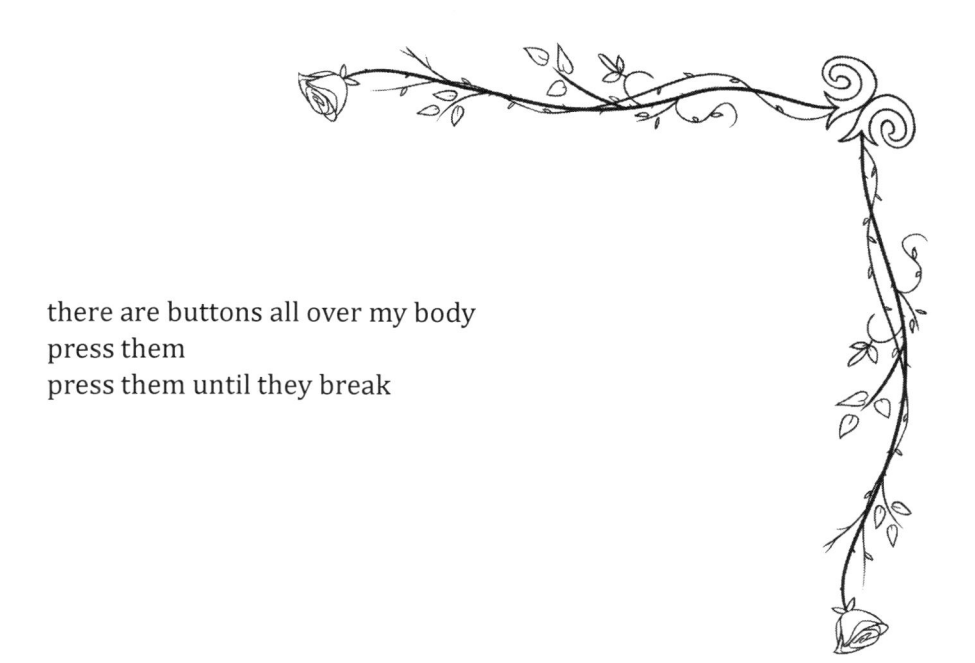

there are buttons all over my body
press them
press them until they break

the only requirement of loving me is that you do it gently
and gently does not mean less than
it simply means softly,
knowingly,
responsibly

just because I write about you
doesn't mean I write for you

when you cut me, does it not feel like you are cutting yourself?
or is it just me that feels everyone else's pain like it's my own?
like I deserve to be torn down
buried in the ground at my feet
simply because I care too much
and feel it all

I have an awful bad habit of running away
and expecting people to follow
like they're attached to my heels
an awful bad habit
far too hopeful and damaging for a girl
who cracks so detrimentally
at the thought of being turned away from

like dandelions turning brittle and translucent as summer
drags, and turns, and ages
I am trying to let go of what once made me feel so full
I'm sure the flowers take no pleasure in dying on the wind
but their loss is necessary for new growth to occur
therefore
my remaking is also necessary for new love to bloom

looking up into clouds
like mountains in the sky
wouldn't it be nice to step above everything
that's causing you so much pain?
wouldn't it be lovely to step right over things like
a broken heart

I imagine being yours so frequently
so secretly

I'm just trying to figure out how to remain soft
in a world that only knows how to be hard

my mother used to tell me
that it hurts to be beautiful
I was sold the belief that beauty came packaged in thorns
and don't be surprised if your hands come away
bloody
smear it on your lips
and smile

what I will tell every blazing sun of a girl around me for the
rest of my life
is that beauty is not pain
beauty is simply there
everywhere
any place you are willing to let light shine

how I wish someone could know me and think:
her freckles are my favourite thing about her
her body is like a mountain range;
messy, beautiful, enough to split the sky
my hands in her hair could hold me for the rest of time
she is a world I never want to stop learning

I don't know what it is to feel wanted
only what it is to want

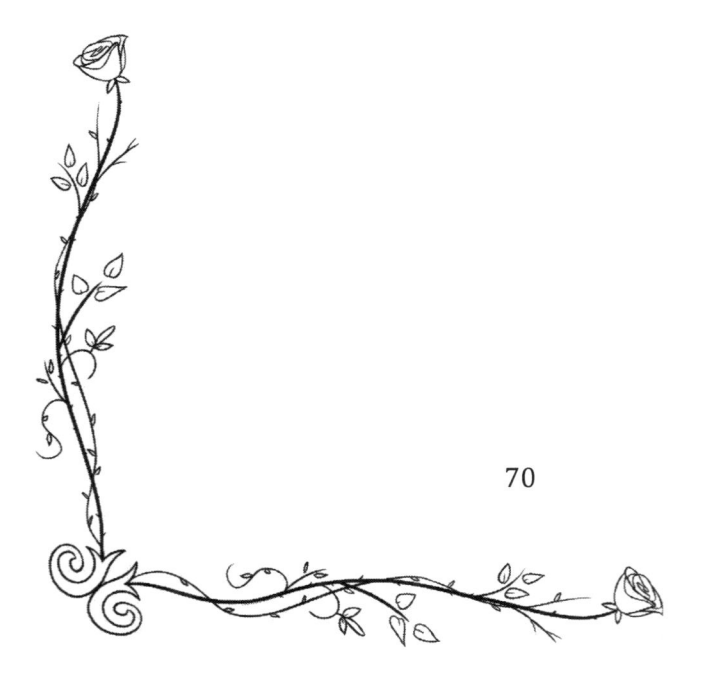

I hate feeling like I need to fling myself off of cliffs
just to see if anyone will follow

I found peace between trees
in slivers of sunlight
in places where the air needed me to breathe
not the other way around

WHOEVER made me think that love and sex were inevitable

did more damage than

whoever made me think that being fat would always stand in the way of being beautiful

did more damage than

whoever made me think that loving myself was selfish and unbecoming

did more damage than

whoever made me think that as a girl I could only have feelings for boys

did more damage than

whoever made me think that my gender was as simple as this. or that.

did more damage than

whoever made me think that it was more important for others to be happy with who I pretended to be rather than me being happy with who I really am

it is ok to want to hold a body made just like your own
it is ok to find comfort in a girl's hands
in the shape of her lips
in the thought of her hips
in the softness of her sweaters
in the sweetness of her letters
girls hold so much love inside of them
infinite and curiously undiscovered
like the universe and the seas
I would trade nothing
for knowing the boundless strength
feeling the glowing tenderness
of a girl's love
it is ok to love girls for the very reasons
they are also called weak
it is ok to love kindness
it is ok to love feather touches
it is ok to love her gentle

(it is even ok to love her before you learn to love yourself)

I wish I was more like the sky after rain;
open and light
there's so much to learn from the sky-
how to shine like the stars
and how to hold happiness like the sun

words
have always buried themselves in me so deep
like knives
I have always twisted them
making beautiful things ugly
changing hello to goodbye
creating wounds out of nothing

I have all but become my words
even the ones I don't speak
even the ones that aren't true
that's what happens when you think too much
and say too little
words have created me
and they let me create
and isn't it terrifying
and beautiful
how much power
they have

here I am falling apart
and you don't even know
that you've got my future in one hand
and my end in the other

words are the best version of me
words love me
words build me
words wreck me
words work wonderfully when I can't find my voice
words are all we have

it's unfairly rare, and so goddamn difficult
but sometimes I can stand to look at myself naked and think
this is right
this is the home I'll never have to leave
this is mine
this body is a bloom, always shedding petals
growing anew
twining into foreign foliage
retreating when conditions get too harsh

I need to remind myself: I love you
you beautiful thing
your fragility has never compromised for the sharpness of
your edges
the possibility of you breaking has never diminished the
beauty of all your pieces

if I had to describe myself in opposites
I would admit that I'm both rough and tender
tender like professing love, easy as breathing
tender like fingers gliding through hair, like rain kissing the
earth
and yet
rough like the old scars on a tired heart
rough like mountains standing through storms that would
obliterate
anything softer

all you have to say is my name and I feel stars shooting around
in my chest
I'm breathing sparks and fire
I'm a second away from burning down every single thing
keeping my lips from
tenderly
roughing
up
yours

she makes a gun with her hand and pulls the trigger
I know exactly where she aims
the thing she hits, she won't destroy
she just wants someone to be found in

she just knows

        (does she know)

she loves kind hearts

        (she has mine)

and gentle hands

        (in hers)

I want to say:

I'm up all night thinking about you anyway, so if you needed someone to talk to at 3 am, I could be her. I can be the girl who loves you the way you want to be loved. I'm already there. I want to be your safe place. My heart feels like it was made to shelter yours.

to see someone you admire
for their confidence
break down in a flood of cold insecurity
stabbing shards of doubt through their own heart
should make you admire them even more
they are human
and they let you see them weak
they are stronger for having let you help them rebuild
this is how we should strive to be with each other
to help sort and scrap and strengthen
the pieces of us

I think that touching you might be like touching a painting
a little forbidden
unquestionably satisfying

tell me what your dreams are
and who you want to be
when you achieve them

you think too much love could break a thing like you
but one day the right love will walk through your doors
turn a different light on each day
blow dust off of one thing at a time
and will know that your heart requires one who treads
carefully

I worry that you think my silence means I don't need you
I worry you'll never know how untrue that is

I want you to know
that you can be soft for me
even when you're hard for the rest of the world

the world gives us no choice

the stardust on my fingertips is proof that I've been reaching
for something better
it means, one day, I'll hold the stars whole

I want to hear the things you never dreamed you'd have the
courage to say aloud
my ears
want to hear
everything
you only ever dared
to whisper to yourself
every echo of your heart
no matter how faint
or how
thunderous

for all the times I wanted to tell someone that they're beautiful
and that they make me happy
and that the world is a better place with them in it:

you're beautiful
you make me happy
the world is a better place because you exist

the positive things are what we will regret holding back the
most

one day you're going to be so happy
and even if it's not with me
I'll feel your happiness like it's my own
because it has always been that way
between me and the people

I have loved,
        love,
                will always love,

half of my heart has always existed outside of myself
completely
out of my control

I think people are like stories
and when they write you into their lives
that's something to be thankful for
even if it's just for a chapter
I'm so glad to have pages with your smile on them

maybe to comfortably read these words
you just have to pretend that they're not about you
but if writing this was uncomfortable for me
should reading it really be comfortable for you?

though I've been hurt
and it feels, sometimes, like the fault is yours
I would never blame you for this:
finding some kind of peace elsewhere
wanting what you couldn't have with me
needing to feel wanted
and letting someone else want you
more completely than I ever could

I have to tell myself that everything will be ok
since you stopped telling me such things

is this what I get for asking for honesty?

since when did loving you become such a sword to fall on?

I don't know how much or how little
truth there is in how I think and feel
I just know that when you said
it would be too hard
to love me from so far
I heard, instead
you're not worth it

do you build yourself?
or do you just fall together?

sometimes poetry is enough
the words are big enough to fill the space
where the things you don't have are missing from

your heart
was like a dark hollow
carved into the trunk of something timeworn and tired
I was never afraid to reach my hands in
but that's not to say that I'm not afraid of the dark
I just
I really thought I was wanted there

sometimes it hurts so bad that all I can think is "holy shit"

Girl
and
Earth
they should not thrum at different frequencies
but still
some things make me feel like my matter
and that of the rest of the world
were never meant
to blend

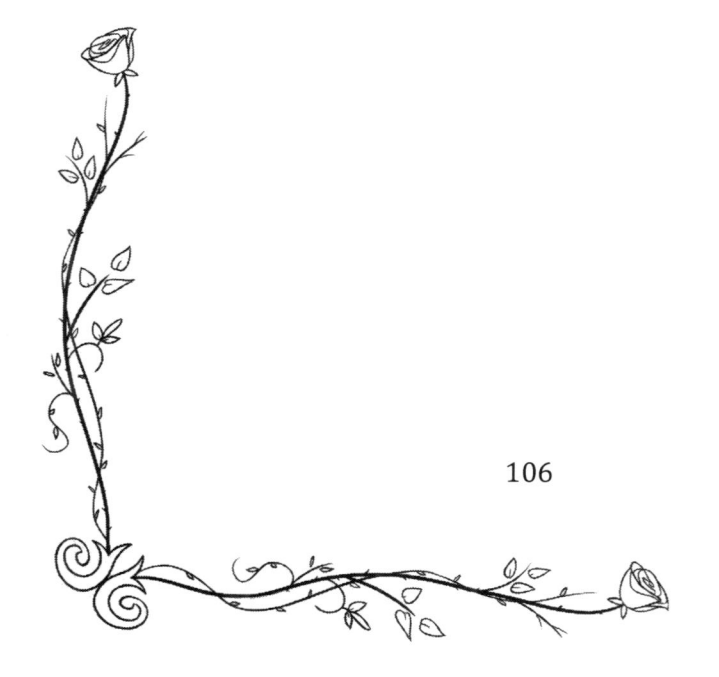

I thought it would be helpful
to practice catharsis
to let it all spill
to loosen the knots
to push off
to finally break
if I just told someone how I felt
but one word out, ten more too late
I wanted to suck the breath back into my body
snatch the words out of the air
because the world is just too harsh a place
a space too cruel for my soft,
broken words
to bleed into

how do I fix this flaw:

that I find it so easy to fall in love
and so hard to tell the truth

heart a wretched place
stomach a quivering mess
all the things I keep on the inside
run around, frantic
there's broken glass in all my limbs
and burnt out lights behind my eyes
how many young people feel older than nightmares?

even though we were quiet
because we were
even though dark things had started to grow between us
because we let them grow
I felt safe falling asleep with you

you make me want to break
my look but don't touch mentality
I've always loved admiring artwork on walls
seeing dreams in someone else's masterpiece
but with you my hands feel like paint brushes
and your body is the softest canvas
beautiful without having been touched
but maybe I could make you feel
just a little bit more
magnificent
than you already are

conversations with my parents

I

I don't want kids. Would you really be mad at me if you didn't have grandchildren?

I would be disappointed, yes. You sound so selfish.

can't

My friend-

Is she big like you?

ever

I hate you

bitch

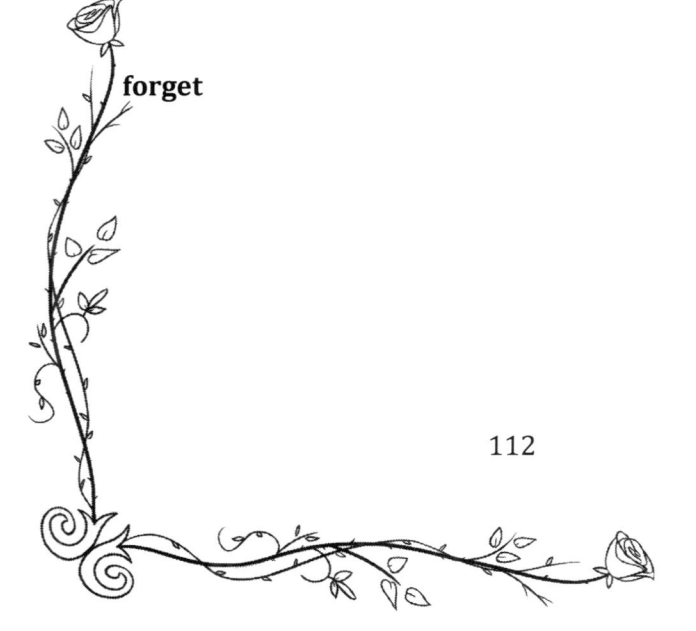

forget

every time you tell me you love me
a cloud bleeds out
and rains its entire self onto our cheeks
to cool our heartbeats
I tell us both
it died to tell you to slow down
when really
its vanishing was as natural as what you give me

I'm always so upside down with feelings that I push away
what's right
and real
and true

I am jealous of the anything that you give to him
the energy, the attention, the compassion
the space in your head and your heart
I am jealous of the anything you give away
to someone that isn't me
because anything that starts out small can grow into
a kind of mountainous, devastating
uncontainable something
I worry that anything you feel will turn into
something
without me there

I've always seen what I can see now
my deliberately turning away
was not the equivalent of unknowing

around the time you stopped picking flowers from
my garden heart
for my sunshine hands
I stopped feeling obligated to watch over
what you had growing so tenderly new
in your own wilds
it started to hurt too much, picking flowers for you
when all the stems grew thorns so big and menacing
cutting myself on them was not the good kind of compromise
it was like burning a forest to the ground just to see the smoke
just to darken something that was once glowing

I hope you at least think of me sometimes
just once in a while
just fleetingly as you get dressed for the day
just passingly as you order your coffee
just warmly as you hear someone else say my name on the
street
I hope you at least think of me a little
while I'm thinking of you a lot
because if not
the universe will be horribly out of balance
all thanks to our own broken scale
always leaning dangerously more into my heart
than yours

love, you might have been a shooting star
just for me
just for a moment
perhaps I unknowingly spoke my wishes out loud because
they never came true
but I'm learning to think of myself as the sun
I'll never turn my light away from you
no amount of wishing
from me or from you
could make me want to leave you cold

love, I'm not fine
just fooling myself
into thinking I can live without
you being mine

all I've heard them say is, "you need to let it go"
what does that even mean?
forget? impossible
pretend to forget? possibly
but how much good do I have to pretend to forget along with
the bad
let go of what's weighing you down
let go of what's causing you pain
let go of what's pushing you to your knees
let go of what's keeping you from growing
let go of what's not holding onto you
let go of what is clearly too much of a burden on your
struggling soul
how do I let you go?
how do I just
let go
of what my hands wanted to hold so badly they shook with
desire
of what made my chaotic heart finally, finally calm
of what my stars told me I needed
again
and again
and again
and still

the people you're almost certain
are too good for you to have deserved
are the ones you have to fight the hardest
to keep
you need them
if only to teach yourself
that you deserve the very best

read the books on your shelf with your mind wide open
read the palms of your hands knowing, under thin skin, lies
your soul
read the gestures of your friends with faithful remembrance
read the stars in the sky
they've been telling us who we are since before we were born
read the world around you and you'll find there is
　　　nothing
　　　　you can't learn

all the feelings of an unfeeling girl
for all the eyes in an unfeeling world
I'll always be scared to show you what I'm made of
but we've all lied in beds we wish we hadn't tried to make love
in every painting on every wall
there is a beauty that makes me feel so wonderfully small
because of all the stories I care ache-deep for
I learn, and learn, and always crave more

Getting to know you, little by little, is one of the most exciting things happening in my life right now. You are so bright to me, so sunshine-y and beautiful, and the image of your smile makes me do the same, uncontrollably. This is just an honest letter to you. My heart finally deviated enough for me to write to someone new.

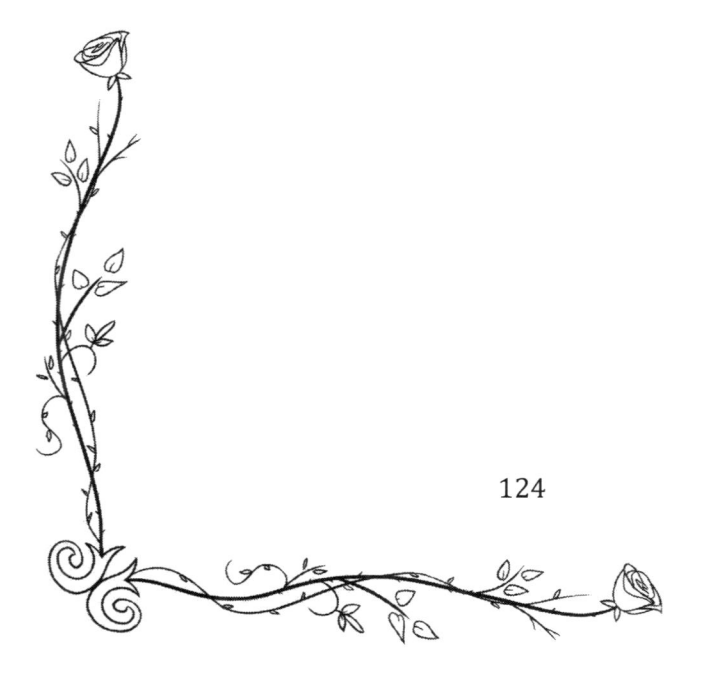

they ask me
do you want to be a writer?
and I think
I would
if only I could write about
anything
other than you

afterthought

people look at me
and do not realize
that they're not looking into a mirror
we are not the same
and we don't have to be

I picked up your words
they were weightless

I might always be saying goodnight
to people I don't owe it to

and you're an oil slick out here in a rainstorm
nothing as pure
as water, as tears
sticks to your bones
not the hate
and especially
not the love

I think you know that I love you
but I don't think you know how much
or how it's not so much a love as a crisis
or how living with it everyday in my heart
makes me so damn confused and lonely
I think you know that I love you
but I don't think you know that it's killing me

I couldn't listen to you telling me how new and strange and
good it felt
for you to get to know his body with your body
I couldn't hear you tell me you loved me without wondering
what you said to him
if anything
with your back on a mattress and him between your legs
I couldn't handle how he left you once he used you
but I handled it so you didn't have to handle it alone

you told me you loved me once
twice
so many times I started to believe it
forgive me if I thought we were more than friends
my mistake, I guess, to love those who only love me by mistake
temporarily
as warm as summer rain, as fleetingly as summer itself

what about my body is virgin?
untouched?
my fingertips have created a language only the insides of my
thighs respond to
I am beautifully experienced without the help of anyone
outside of
myself

I think the reason we don't depend on the sound of the other's
voice
or the sight of the other's face
or the feel of the other's body
is because
I fell in love with you through words
I feel you in everything you write
I hear it loud and clear
it moves me to tears
it started with words
it could end there too
there's nothing cold about loving you like this

the hardest thing I've ever had to do?
I haven't done it yet
I haven't quit you

I say that confessing love
for me
that's just not easy
yet it tumbles out of my mouth for you daily
so which is it?
I asked my heart
she said
I think our mouth got tired of keeping all our words in
I think our head got sick of pretending I'm not the one calling
the shots
I think caring too much made us mince the affection we show
to others
and I think telling people their worth is immeasurable
is one hell of a way
to feel alive

I never felt more beautiful than when she said it
through the wire
across the stars
she didn't even know me
but she made me feel as real as houses
as whole as heaven

*asexual

would the world know what to do
with all the poems I could write
about loving myself at night
at 2 am
with a hand on my breast
and a hand having sex
and a fever slicking it all
with sweat
would the world know what to do
with an innocent* girl
who loves her own moans
so much so
she may only ever gift them to herself

is that a rib?
my fingers push into the fat 1 2 3 4 inches s o f t
a body as big as mine still bruises
do I even have bones?
face neck chest
always rounded out never caving in
I've never seen a clavicle anywhere
except on every beautiful person
I would die to just try one on
whatever will make those shadows appear
(I want to look a little hidden)
do skeletons like jewellery?
no matter how I rotate my wrist I can't see the pisiform
I know how bracelets can clang against the jut
I've just never been that type of delicate
who would hold this hand?
it wears size 8 rings and the knuckles are more like dimples
when I say soft I mean the inside of a rose I don't mean
all this flesh
how sharp is bone really?
I've been thinking about the zygomatic arch
how mine's no curve. no contour. no sharpness. no beauty.

fat girls teach themselves all the names of the bones thin girls
wear
on the outside of their bodies

some would do anything to wear their insides on their
outsides
if it made them a little easier on the eyes

isn't that beautiful?

I want to wake up inhaling the air electric crisp and lively
lovely side effects of living palm to palm with nature
I want to share this life with someone whose dreams are
crowded canvases
waiting to step into the world and paint it lustrously new
aiming to wash away the loudness, the loneliness
I want to celebrate every precious little minute we are lucky to
live
on a planet of shimmering seas and goddess green
in a galaxy layered in starlight
in a space so vivid lush and endless
I want to spend the mornings clutching notebooks and pens
and each other's hands
loosening our limits until nothing large is impossible

I think a part of me will always put you first
but I think other parts of me are fine with moving on
can being torn apart
really be the only way to be whole again?

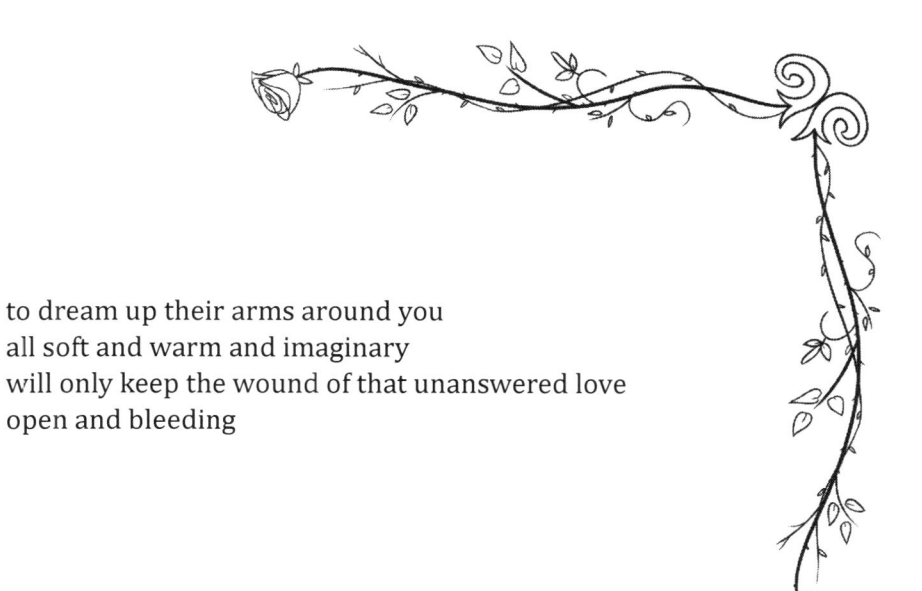

to dream up their arms around you
all soft and warm and imaginary
will only keep the wound of that unanswered love
open and bleeding

For now, it doesn't matter how often or how truthfully I claim to be moved on from what we shared. It doesn't matter because, maybe forever, you are who is in my mind for every love poem I read. It doesn't matter if it's about how good love feels, how painful it is when it ends, how destructive it is when it breaks, how gentle it is when it's with you. Your face and your hands and your smile and your body will never leave my mind no matter how far away from love we may move.

there I go again
I went and fell in love
who knows for how long
it doesn't matter
all I know is that their name tastes like
cookies in my mouth
and the thought of them washes my mind
clean

it was
the give and take
of us
that finally thinned me out
to nothing
to a wispy collection
of broken threads

actually

it was not the give and take of us
it was the consistency of my giving
and your taking

and then

it was the consistency of my giving
and your not wanting
anymore

and then

it was the consistency of my giving
the unrelenting of my beaten up
heart
and your back turned to me
finally

for me
for you
for us
for alternate, alternate universes
where maybe all of our decisions were made differently
and when we reached out our hands
they found the same something solid
to hold onto
- I'm happy for that me, for that you, for that us

Acknowledgments

Buddy Fan Club; Maddy, Zoey, Chandra (and Buddy). Thank you all for being such thoughtful and supportive friends–always talking like it was entirely possible for me to be a published author one day even though I was composed of 95% doubt.

Shanda and Emily. Thank you for being among the very few people I ever trusted enough to share my words with, to be myself with. You both invented being kind and supportive and non-judgemental.

Iz. Thank you for your beautiful artwork. Thank you for understanding exactly what I wanted, for making that cover girl me, but not me. Thank you for your sweetness and encouragement.

Maria. Thank you for swooping in and saving me from formatting hell. Also, thank you for caring so much, and being so vocal about sapphic lit/poetry- to work with someone who values lgbtqiap+ content as much as you do has been a pleasure and means a lot to me.

Libby. Thank you, my love, for always being there for me, for giving me a million *hugs* and *kisses*, for being such a beautiful inspiration. Thanks for taking up so much space in my heart, for being the spark that made this whole thing burn, for being the water that put out all the flames. You are infinitely special to me. If we're not together in this life, we're together in the next (as cats, of course).

Every single reader out there. Thank you. Thank you so much. It means the world to me, that anyone could enjoy what I have to write. It means the universe to me, that anyone could relate to my words and feel less alone, less unknown.

About the Author

Shelby Eileen is a Canadian writer in a perpetual state of stress concerning her unmapped future. She studied at Brock University where she acquired a bachelor's degree in English Language and Literature. Her lifelong love of reading is what encouraged her to study words in all their meanings, movements, and genres. Publishing her first work has been a scary but liberating step toward hopefully sharing more of her words with the world someday. Connect with her on twitter @briseisbooks.

Printed in Great Britain
by Amazon